Wilf had a cat.
He put a hat on the cat.

KU-433-917

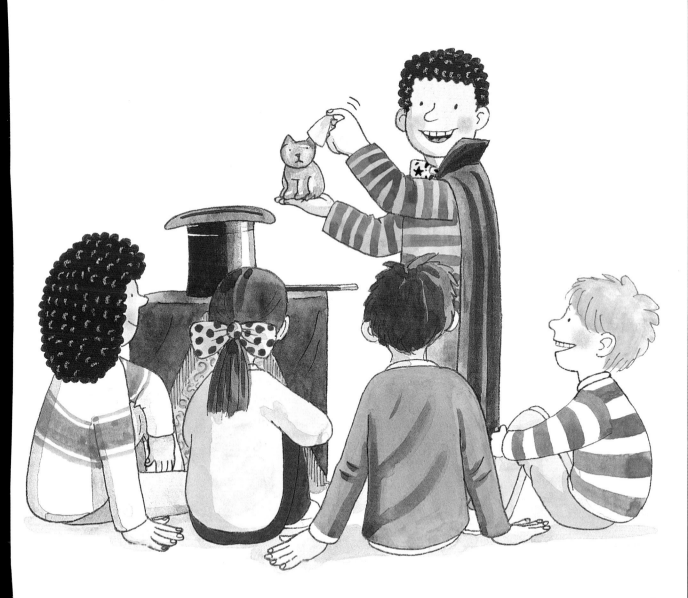

Wilf had a bag.
He put the cat in the bag.

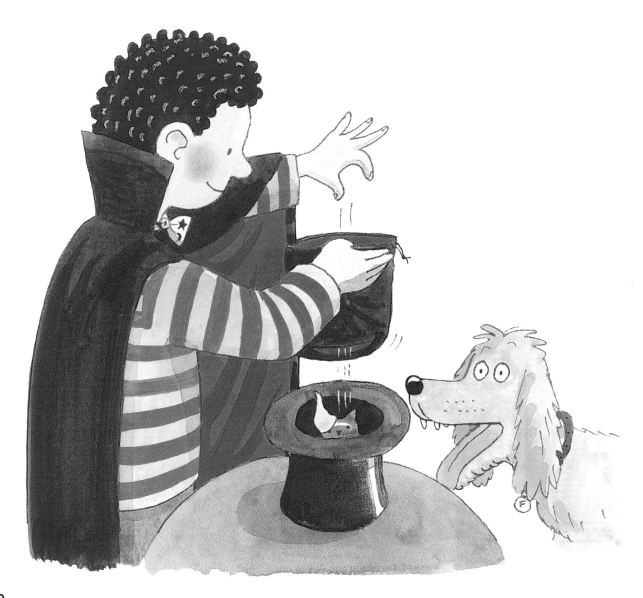

2

tap, tap, tap

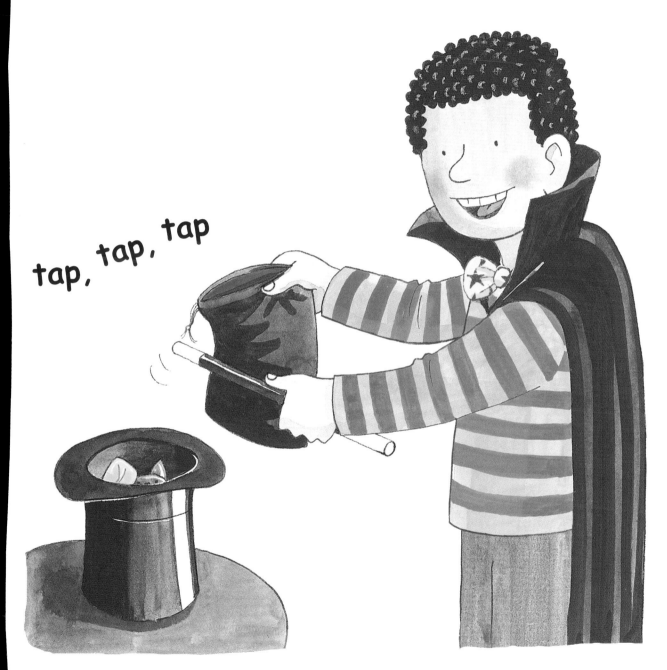

3

Wilf had a tub.
He put the bag in the tub.

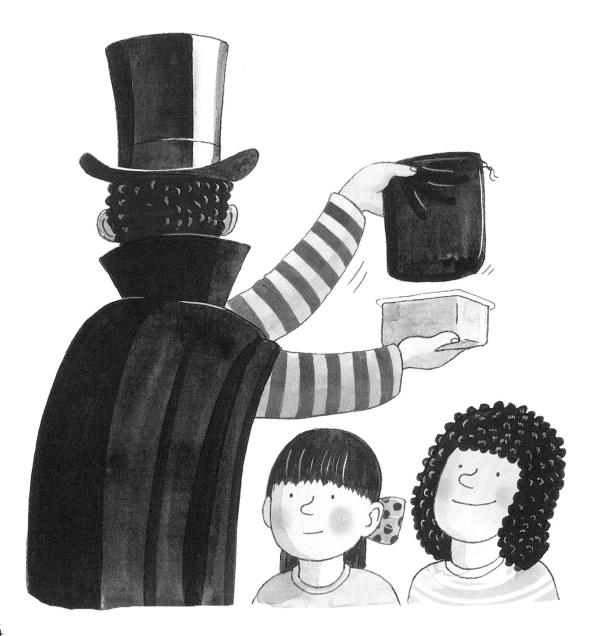

tap, tap, tap

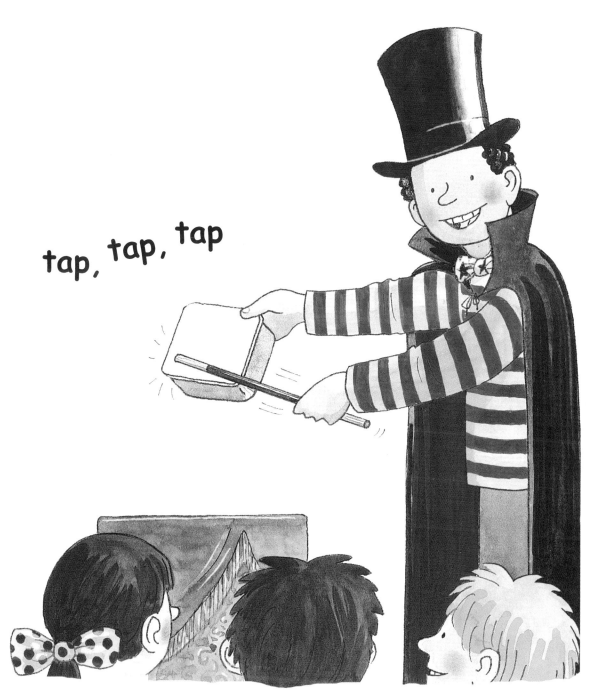

Wilf had a tin.
He put the tub in the tin.

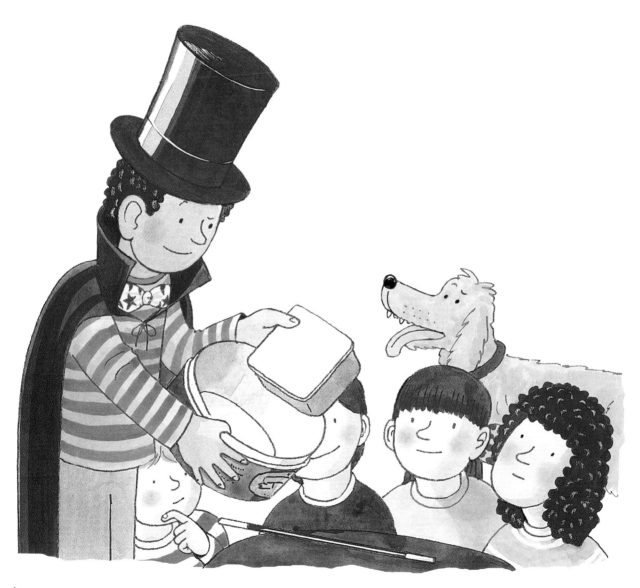

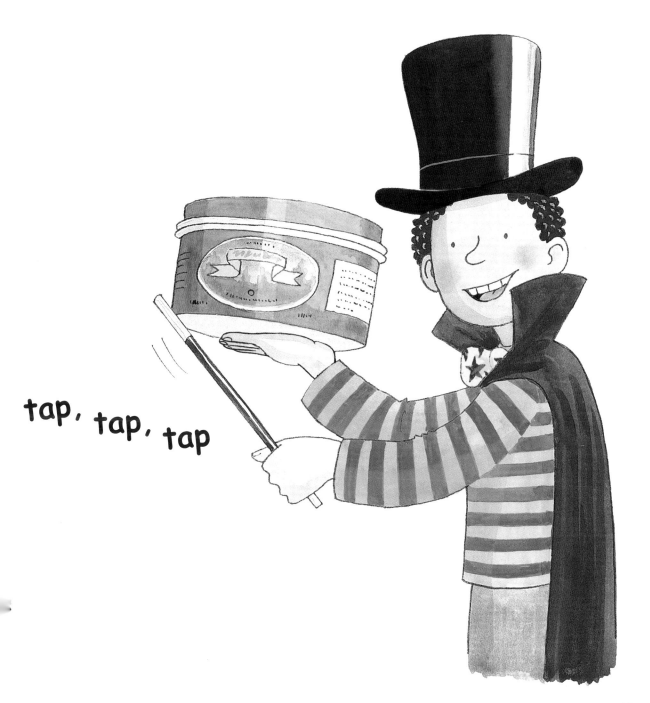

tap, tap, tap

Wilf had the cat in his hat.

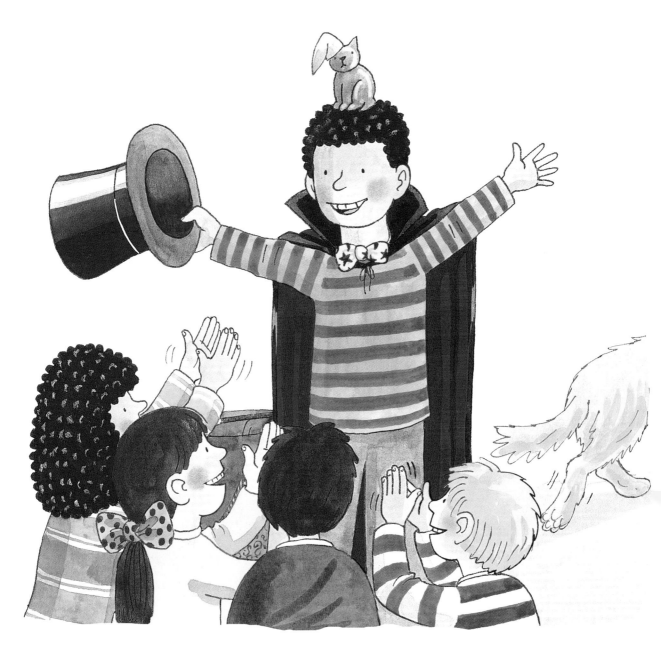